I SPY

SPOOKY NIGHT

A BOOK OF PICTURE RIDDLES

Photographs by Walter Wick

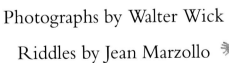

Riddles by Jean Marzollo

Cartwheel
·B·O·O·K·S·®

SCHOLASTIC INC.

New York   Toronto   London   Auckland   Sydney
Mexico City   New Delhi   Hong Kong   Buenos Aires

For Nathan and Matt Goodell

———

W. W.

For Luisa, Lily, and Julia

———

J. M.

Book design by Carol Devine Carson

Text copyright © 1996 by Jean Marzollo.
Photographs copyright © 1996 by Walter Wick.
All rights reserved. Published by Scholastic Inc.

SCHOLASTIC, CARTWHEEL BOOKS, and associated logos
are trademarks and/or registered trademarks of Scholastic Inc.

Library of Congress Cataloging-in-Publication Data

Wick, Walter.
    I spy spooky night: a book of picture riddles / photographs by
Walter Wick; riddles by Jean Marzollo.
      p.   cm.
    Summary: Rhyming verses ask readers to find hidden objects in
the photographs.
    ISBN 0-590-48137-1
    [1. Picture puzzles — Juvenile literature.]   I. Marzollo, Jean.
II. Title.
    GV1507.P47W529   1996
    793.73'5 — dc20   95-50528
                                                        CIP
                                                        AC

Reinforced Library Edition
ISBN-13: 978-0-439-68429-3
ISBN-10: 0-439-68429-3

10 9 8   9 10 11/0

Printed in Malaysia   46
This edition, March 2005

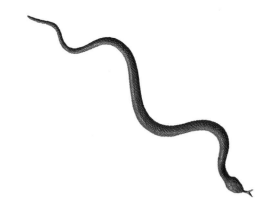

TABLE OF CONTENTS

Picture riddles fill this book;
Turn the pages! Take a look!

Use your mind, use your eye;
Read the riddles — play I SPY!

I spy a broken bone and—BOO!
A padlock, and 1892;

A train, a chain, a busted seam,
An eye of stone, and a silent SCREAM.

I spy four pumpkins, a ruler, a bat,
Eight pinecones, a ladder, three acorns, a cat;

A scarecrow, a key, a clothespin, a clock,
Two bowling pins, and KNOCK, KNOCK, KNOCK!

11

I spy a swan, a turtle, a bear,
A lizard, MOM, and a bone repair;

Four owls, a yardstick, a spool, a comb,
BEWARE, a mouse, and ANYBODY HOME?

13

I spy a beetle, a snake in the grass,
One dozen ants, two birdies of brass;

Eight hands, a frog, a seafaring bird,
A spider, twin ducks, and a backward word.

I spy a crayon, a dinosaur lamp,
TICK TOCK TICK, an eagle, a stamp;

Three nails, three springs, a wishbone, a four,
And a string that hangs from a hidden door.

I spy an X, four spiders, a cat,
Two kids with a dog, WORKSHOP, a bat;

A candle that's old, a candle that's new,
And a big red box with a rebus clue.

19

I spy a shark, three bats, and a map,
Two paddles, an anchor, a red bottle cap;

An egg that is cracked, a rabbit, a three,
A bowling pin stone, and a skeleton key.

I spy a clothespin, a short sad poem,

A magnet, a mouse, a little palindrome;

Three corks, a spool, a black cat spout,
A whistle, a wagon, a whale, and WATCH OUT!

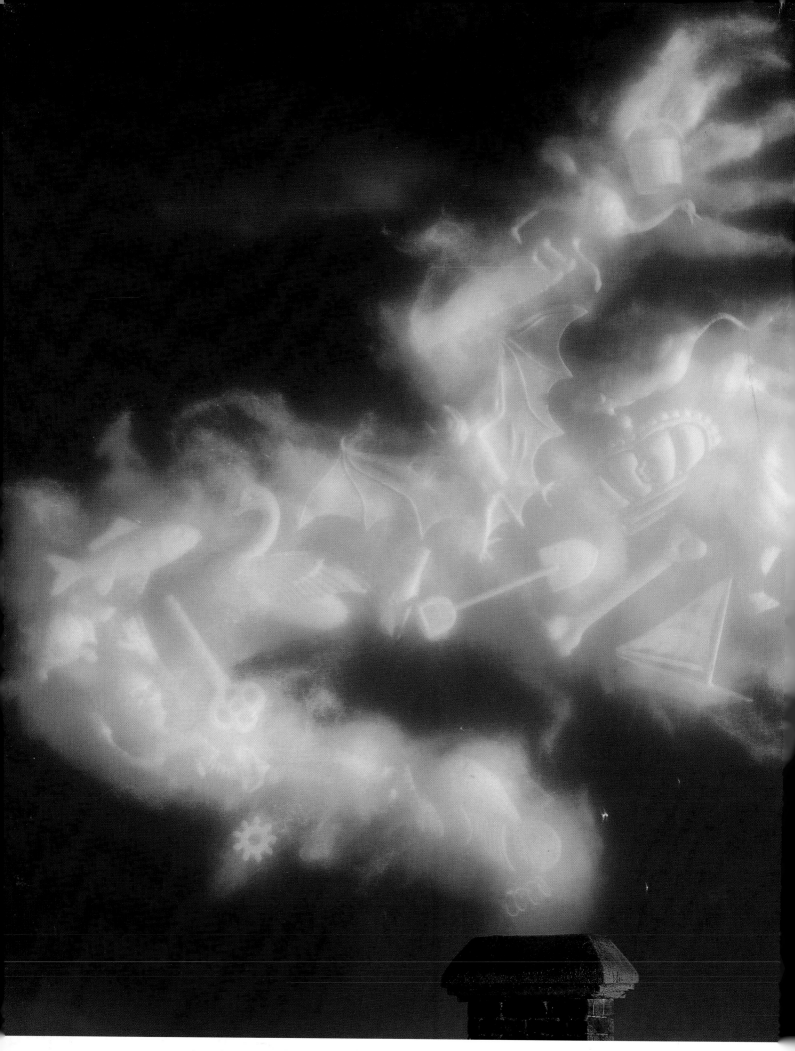

I spy a ladder, pliers, a nail,
Three fish, a swan, and a ghostly sail;

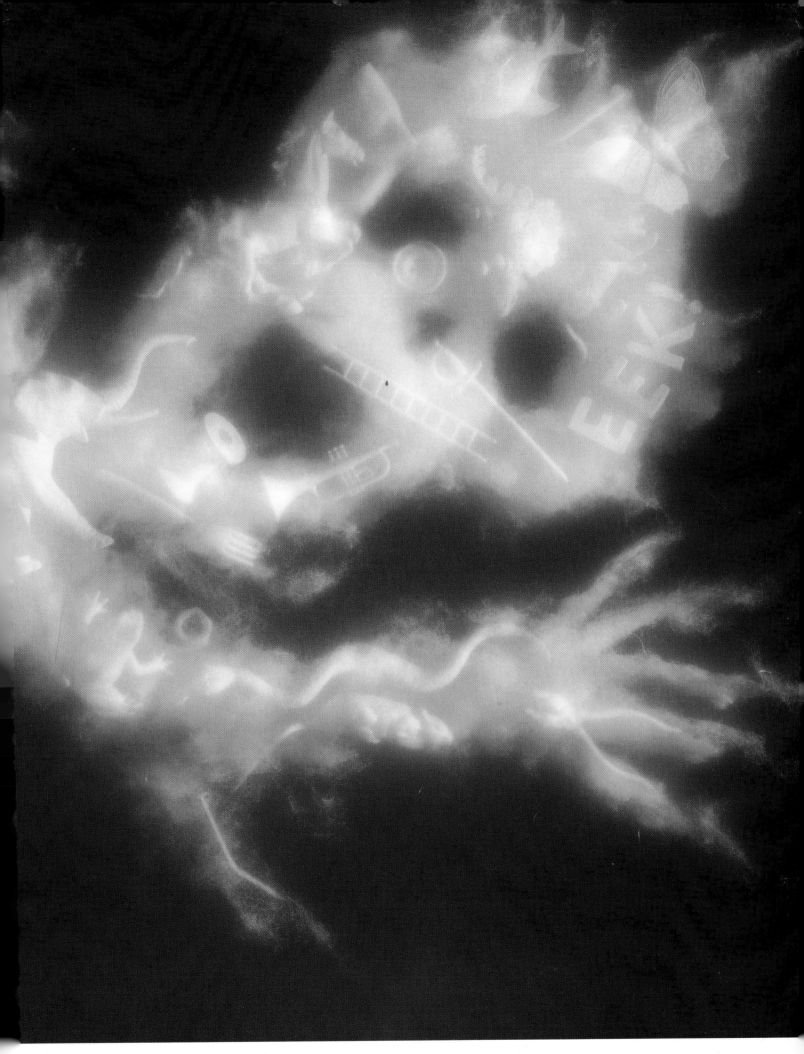

A trumpet, a shovel, an ostrich beak,
Two mice, a sword, a snake, and EEK!

I spy an owl, a lizard, a mouse,

A spider, three swans, a pig, a house;

A knife, a fork, an apple, some rope,
A race car, a shoe, and a brass telescope.

I spy a saddle, six rabbits, a rose,
A seahorse, a windmill, and two dominoes;

Nine birds, a paintbrush, a little blue bow;
A feather, a fan, and an old radio.

I spy a knight, a lion, a dime,
A spoon, a moon, and ONCE upon a TIME.

A cat with stripes, a key on a chair,
Two robots, a phone, and ENTER IF YOU DARE.

EXTRA CREDIT RIDDLES

"Find Me" Riddle

In every scene with bones of white

I'm a _____ on a spooky night.

Find the Pictures That Go With These Riddles:

I spy a paintbrush, a horseshoe, a shell,

An octopus, dragonfly, goose, and a bell.

I spy five birds, a small safety pin,

A pinecone, a spring, and a pumpkin's grin.

I spy a skunk, scissors, a spoon,

A rolling pin, and a man in the moon.

I spy a toothbrush, a baseball, a car,

A seagull, a clothespin, LOVE, and a star.

I spy a bat, a button, a horse,

A white butterfly, and a turtle, of course.

I spy a rabbit, two hammers, a fox,
Glasses, a cage, and a polka-dot box.

I spy a boot, a lantern, a ship,
A moon, a mask, and an old paper clip.

I spy a yardstick, a windmill, two clocks,
Four checkers, two ladders, and a pair of socks.

I spy a glove, a ruler, a knight,
A shoe, a key, and a silver flashlight.

I spy two turtles, a horseshoe, a bone,
A fly, a snake, and a spooky gravestone.

I spy a fly and a bowling pin,
A turtle, a pig, and a violin.

I spy a seahorse, a closed safety pin,
A sword, and a snake that has no skin.

What Is a Rebus? A Palindrome?

In a rebus, pictures stand for words—for example, an eyeball for "I," a heart for "love," and a U for "you." A palindrome reads the same backward and forward—for example, WOW.

Write Your Own Spooky Stories

What scary stories can you make up to go with the pictures in this book? Use your imagination. There are no "right" answers — so be creative! Try telling the story from four different points of view: the person entering the haunted house, the skeleton, the original owner of the house, and the child who owns the dollhouse.

The Story of *I Spy Spooky Night*

Jean Marzollo and Walter Wick receive many suggestions from children for new *I Spy* books. One of the most frequently offered ideas was for a spooky *I Spy* book so Ms. Marzollo and Mr. Wick set about imagining how the book would work. This would be the first *I Spy* book with a plot. But a plot needs a main character — who would that be?

Ms. Marzollo and Mr. Wick resolved that, as in all of the *I Spy* books, the main character would remain the reader who accepts the challenge of solving the picture riddles. In *I Spy Spooky Night,* however, the reader also dares to enter a haunted house. Beckoned from room to room by a trickster skeleton, the reader/hero explores the scary dream environment of a spooky night. Brave heroes seek challenge; as they solve the riddles, they master the fears of night, one page at a time. With dawn comes relief, a relief that lasts only as long as the reader wants—before beginning the book again.

How *I Spy Spooky Night* Was Made

Walter Wick created the elaborate sets for *I Spy Spooky Night* in his studio and then photographed them with an 8" by 10" view camera. The sets vary in size. Clues to their actual dimensions are provided by ordinary objects and toys: a baseball, a yardstick, a candle, a crayon. To make the haunted house, Mr. Wick altered a Victorian dollhouse. He lit the interior and painted a spooky sky for a backdrop. The gates, the rooms, and the outside scenes were carefully constructed with wood, styrofoam, cloth, toys, dry ice, cotton, household objects, and dollhouse props.

The spooky tree in the graveyard shot was made from a blueberry bush, to which Mr. Wick added and subtracted branches until he achieved the dramatic look he wanted. Each finished set was lit by Mr. Wick to create the right shadows, depth, and mood. When the final photograph was made, the set was dismantled.

Acknowledgments

We extend a special thanks to Bruce Morozko for his artistry, expertise, and help in the construction of the sets for *The Empty Hall, A Blazing Fire, The Library, Discovery in the Graveyard,* and *The Fountain.* We are grateful for the patience and dedication of Dan Helt, Walter Wick's assistant through-out the entire project, and for the contributions of Lee Hitt, Krista Borst, Maria McGowan, Rick Schwab, The Tor-rington Doll House, and the unfailing support of Linda Cheverton-Wick. We appreciate the continued assistance of Grace Maccarone, Bernette Ford, Edie Weinberg, Angela Biola, and many others at Scholastic. Last, we thank our agent Molly Friedrich at Aaron Priest Agency for her wise guidance.

Walter Wick and Jean Marzollo

How the *I Spy* Books Are Made

Jean Marzollo and Walter Wick together conceive the ideas for the *I Spy* books. As the sets are constructed, Mr. Wick and Ms. Marzollo confer by phone and fax on objects to go in the sets, selecting things for their rhyming potential, as well as their aesthetic, playful, and educational qualities. The final riddles are written upon completion of the final photographs.

Walter Wick, the inventor of many photographic games for *Games* magazine, is the photographer of *I Spy: A Book of Picture Riddles, I Spy Christmas, I Spy Fun House, I Spy Mystery, I Spy Fantasy,* and *I Spy School Days*. He is also a freelance photographer credited with over 300 magazine and book covers, including *Newsweek, Discover, Psychology Today,* and Scholastic's *Let's Find Out* and *SuperScience*. Mr. Wick graduated from the Paier Art School in New Haven, Connecticut. This is his seventh book for Scholastic. He is also working on a science book of photographs for children called *A Drop of Water*.

Jean Marzollo, a graduate of the Harvard Graduate School of Education, has written many children's books including the *I Spy* books, *In 1492, In 1776, Ten Cats Have Hats, Snow Angel, Sun Song, Pretend You're a Cat,* and *Close Your Eyes*. She is also the author of *My First Book of Biographies* and *Happy Birthday, Martin Luther King*. **Carol Devine Carson**, the book designer for the *I Spy* series, is an art director for a major publishing house in New York City. For 19 years Ms. Marzollo and Ms. Carson produced Scholastic's kindergarten magazine, *Let's Find Out*.

I Spy Books for All Ages:
I SPY: A BOOK OF PICTURE RIDDLES
I SPY CHRISTMAS
I SPY EXTREME CHALLENGER!
I SPY FANTASY
I SPY FUN HOUSE
I SPY GOLD CHALLENGER!
I SPY MYSTERY
I SPY SCHOOL DAYS
I SPY SPOOKY NIGHT
I SPY SUPER CHALLENGER!
I SPY TREASURE HUNT
I SPY ULTIMATE CHALLENGER!
I SPY YEAR-ROUND CHALLENGER!

Books for New Readers:
SCHOLASTIC READER LVL 1: I SPY A BALLOON
SCHOLASTIC READER LVL 1: I SPY A BUTTERFLY
SCHOLASTIC READER LVL 1: I SPY A CANDY CANE
SCHOLASTIC READER LVL 1: I SPY A DINOSAUR'S EYE
SCHOLASTIC READER LVL 1: I SPY A PENGUIN
SCHOLASTIC READER LVL 1: I SPY A PUMPKIN
SCHOLASTIC READER LVL 1: I SPY A SCARY MONSTER
SCHOLASTIC READER LVL 1: I SPY A SCHOOL BUS
SCHOLASTIC READER LVL 1: I SPY FUNNY TEETH
SCHOLASTIC READER LVL 1: I SPY LIGHTNING IN THE SKY
SCHOLASTIC READER LVL 1: I SPY SANTA CLAUS

And for the Youngest Child:
I SPY LITTLE ANIMALS
I SPY LITTLE BOOK
I SPY LITTLE BUNNIES
I SPY LITTLE CHRISTMAS
I SPY LITTLE LEARNING BOX
I SPY LITTLE LETTERS
I SPY LITTLE NUMBERS
I SPY LITTLE WHEELS

Also Available:
I SPY CHALLENGER FOR GAME BOY ADVANCE
I SPY JUNIOR: PUPPET PLAYHOUSE CD-ROM
I SPY JUNIOR CD-ROM
I SPY SCHOOL DAYS CD-ROM
I SPY SPOOKY MANSION CD-ROM
I SPY TREASURE HUNT CD-ROM